Thought Splinters

the thoughts of man reflect his actions

Fiction Today
Reality Tomorrow

by
Thor Molen

DORRANCE PUBLISHING CO., INC.
PITTSBURGH, PENNSYLVANIA 15222

ISBN # 0-8059-3525-8
Printed in the United States of America

First Printing

For information or to order additional books, please write:
Dorrance Publishing Co., Inc.
643 Smithfield Street
Pittsburgh, Pennsylvania 15222
U.S.A.

Preface

Finally something different...a challenge to bring knowledge into art...a better form of education.

This may be the answer to keeping pace with the growth of our knowledge and giving us the peace of mind we crave. Life represents an order—out of disorder, anarchism. Life was created to follow rules, to fulfill happiness and satisfaction. It is our choice as observers to search and look for satisfaction in art, that it may give us a pleasant experience to motivate our actions.

We are in desperate need for more correct forms of communication. Our language and number systems furnish us with knowledge to make us smart or intelligent. The broadness of word power, the number of words and understanding correctly their meanings, reflects man's standards among man. Another way to recognize the world.

But the world is in a state of movement in all directions. We need a stationary physic to build directions. We need a stationary physic to build houses, streets, cars, airplanes, etc., but also to form the action of our minds—this needs a different way to recognize the world. Please take my pictures as a forecast in the direction to force our minds to recognize our moveable world more correctly.

For protection man built walls, but to understand the use of tools
is the power of man. He learns to use them loosely, put together
like collected fieldstones or well-fitted through schooling like brick
walls. But tools create a man made world, through communication,
observation, and judgment.

In definite chances we receive life, well-filtered, only screened
come to life. Between birth and death we leave mysteries for outsiders.

This book represents a collection of "thought splinters" as they occur in daily life; an introduction to motivate the reader to think. In this process we suggest that meditation be used to enhance understanding, to compare personal experience and happenings, and to concentrate on establishing our own conclusions based on correct judgment. In every few lines there is concentrated knowledge to be found which can only be understood by repeated reading.

Prepare to experience life more correctly. The experiences will form a key in your hand that will give you good health, happiness, and satisfaction—you may recognize the power behind all things. The forces are called God, the Superior Entity, Custodian of the Laws of Nature, and more. Matter and anti-matter (speed or movement in all directions), the creative forces concentrated in dimensions to form a cycle from the absolute minimum in action to the absolute minimum coming to rest. In that state of passing through these states, acting and reacting forces build and form our world of existence.

It is difficult to understand, to break through the man-made mantle of our life that surrounds us and prompts us to accept pre-fabricated conclusions or evidence.

We travel on the surface of the earth at the same speed and we become relatively stationary to each other, so that we develop physical and mathematical rules, working from a stationary base to create our own *world*. If we wish to comprehend the genesis of our moving world, we have to redefine our physical and mathematical rules.

Just three companions of an influential executive.

Introduction

Time and the Future
A Hypothesis

Mankind must separate its reasoning from the traditional linear method, as we exist in an interplay of motion that cannot be simply expressed in lineal projections. In reality we have realized an impasse in our progress, having gone the limit in singular (or linear) "thinking" that results in deductions that will no longer serve to meet any significant progress toward our future betterment. We have based our sciences on preconceived theorems that suffice in themselves, but do not meet the demands that future rationalizing will impose. Several "knowns" tempt the Revisionists in our thinking to seek other forms of communication than those we have thus far employed. Two "knowns" are gravity and time, both which are in actuality still "unknowns." We confuse the *product* of gravity and the *effect* of time with their sources; neither of which we have any concept of as yet. We know the effects of electro-motion but do not know its source, only that it results from certain natural or artificial actions.

Our sciences are taught on mental "rails" that are fatally limited. We teach by repetition instead of by stimulating original thought that can be pursued simultaneously by both professors and students. After a series of repetitive drills, we award certificates to our youth that serve no productive purpose toward expansion of intellect in the sciences or the arts.

Communication is the key to moving intellect to higher levels of achievement. It is in the field of communication that we must first innovate. Language as we know it is self-limited. Art is the universal language that all can understand. An example is the painting on the previous page.

Depicted in this picture is an air-raid shelter sign, which in itself projects any number of illusions which if reduced to the printed word would be prohibitive to complete. The painting is not merely linear but multi-dimensional in concept, though it is necessarily presented on one plane. It exists in various dimensions to astute observers, with each observer employing a personally developed mode of reasoning to arrive at his or her interpretation. A written mathematical or chemical equation will not allow that much latitude of thought. We consider flying to be more difficult than surface movement because it is performed in three instead of two planes of reference. Time is the sum of all planes of reference or better expressed as vectors and not merely the linear expressions in two dimensions that we can easily visualize. Science must strive to develop a multi-directional form of expression and communication to progress. Only then can we begin to answer the many riddles of our existence and discover new and more exciting vistas. We must revise our methods of education that have become outmoded and are self-limited. We have allowed an inertia in our thinking that must be overcome. This cannot be done by continuing to employ the customary methods of communication expressed by the same centuries honored and seemingly sacrosanct mathematical, chemical, geometrical, and other traditional equations, formulas, or theorems. License is assumed here to suggest tangible mediums of expanded communication, one being *art* with paintings of substance that offer variances in interpretation that the aforementioned do not accomplish. Interpretive art offers what may be referred to as "thought vectors" that would result in new concepts and avenues of communication. Art, like music, is a universal mode of expression whose true potential has yet to be explored.

Time, the subtle governor of all known activity, will ultimately be extensively defined and employed in a much different scope than heretofore permitted in scientific conjecture. Mathematics, physics, and chemistry will evolve into new and previously unknown methodology, meaning a more expansive communication and expression in scientific theory and subsequent exploration and development.

Mankind has yet to reach the threshold of development that is possible with omni-directional approaches to scientific thought that respond to the true nature of time. The reasoning process must be altered and separated from emotional forms of motivation that are self-limiting and mask abstract, logical thought. Conversion to this new concept will be difficult and certainly revolutionary in nature. Political solutions will not be effective where the ultimate domination of one society over another is the motivating force. A collateral approach will be necessary, possibly after a unity of most, if not all, worldly states. Logic indicates that such an all-encompassing unity will not be possible unless some global occurrence forces it. With environmental problems developing at present, a scenario whereby unity of effort would be needed is becoming increasingly possible. An example is the questionable condition of the earth's ozone layer as it relates to solar heating. There are others evident tot he discerning observer.

Let us return again to consider *time* in other precepts that we tend to overlook. Any action in our everyday life is a functional series of "time vectors" and said action is absolutely governed by them. We merely have to look at our physical existence to note that we are an extremely complex orchestration of so-called "time vectors." Breath, blood oxygenation, digestion, and our many other daily functions within our physical selves are governed and created, utilized, and eliminated by functions in time. We can easily look elsewhere to such common objects as the internal combustion engine and many others.

In summary: Understanding the true nature and functions of time in pre-existing conditions and defining time in a universally accepted mode of expression is the key to new creative theories which when successfully employed will liberate mankind in a scope never before anticipated. Abstract, unhampered logic liberated from the hindrances of our various emotions must be pursued. Such a dogged direction assumed, as possibly some yet unknown necessity may require, may not set well with politicians and theologians. Progress into an exhilarating and rewarding future will exact a very substantial premium, one which our successors must be willing to pay (John 8:32).

Thor Molen

Part 1

Man is generally accepted as a selfish creation. To keep himself alive, he tries only the easiest ways. When man learns to organize his actions in a form that can bring to others happiness and satisfaction and a successful form of life, he becomes a representative of humanity. Man lives through action and by doing so man becomes H-U-M-A-N.

We exist in a world of movement. Gravity forms movement. Time is the contrasting difference of movements. Time forms contradicting movements on the difference of (a), (b), and (c), or matter. Contradicting movements from imagination. The difference of (a), (b), and (c) forms memory. But most is controlled by the power of communication (anti-matter). All together, this is creativity and it builds our man-made world.

To understand the above, we have to learn to understand dimensions. We exist in dimensions. The first dimension is movement, gravity, and much more. The second dimension is time or the contradicting movement on matter. The third dimension is space. The fourth dimension forms communication or is the dimension of antimatter. The fifth dimension is creativity from a splinter of thought to a product with the help of energies. The sixth dimension is life. The seventh dimension forms destruction or the power of changes.

Time can be recognized as transmission of the difference between movement to non-movement or less movement, forming the creations in our universe. We live through our deeds and we can become immortal with the quality of our accomplishments. These we have to leave behind when we change to the original of our existence, back to the power of life—what we call *death*.

The basis for success in life is self-discipline, correct judgment, and patience.

The instructors for education are gliders. By the use of the freedom we experience in the atmosphere, we form people into personalities for outstanding leadership.

The educational foundation is the power to recognize and understand time. Time is the contradicting movements on the difference of matter. Contradicting movements can be recognized in the action and counteraction in our atmosphere. For glider pilots, the different form of matter is the aircraft. With the help of gravity, inertia, and centrifugal forces, we are capable of controlling the aircraft in a three-dimensional framework for achievements.

We learn to fly and when we do, we fly time. Contradicting movements are represented in our imagination and the different forms of matter can be established in our memory. The mixture of both is the guidance for the value of our expected form of life.

Let us recognize the accomplishments man produced by the discoveries through science in the last two hundred years. These discoveries were mostly reached by the use of physics or mathematics and several more scientific practices.

Man should never forget that we travel on the surface of the earth with the same speed and we become relatively stationary to each other. We form our conclusions to understand our universe from a stationary recognition. But we can learn to understand that we live in an existence of movements, that the difference of movements formed us into what we are.

How many movements is man capable of understanding and using? Movements in all directions at the same time?

We have to learn to think and try to personally understand the power of difference which controls and influences our existence. Mixed with common sense, the dimensions that represent antimatter will or can give us the power of wisdom. Based on common sense, it results in unlimited discoveries. *Thinking* means a collection of evidence out of the past, correctly analyzed to form a future.

We have to learn to understand this, for life movement in all directions at the same time is the power of our existence.

The seven dimensions in which man exists: movement, time, space, communication, life, destruction, or that form creativity.

Thought should be the base that forms the products out of communication. It represents the fourth dimension.

- What is thought?

- A product of thought is supposed to be action.

- Thought is the combination of future and past created in the present.

- Imagination, fiction, and fantasy represent the future, a reaction toward energies.

- Memory, inherited or stored through learning and experience, represents the past.

- Life's deeds in word or action represent the present.

- Put all together, it is the fourth dimension.

To understand the fourth dimension, we have to recognize that by traveling on the surface of the earth we become relatively stationary to each other. So we developed physical and mathematical rules working from a stationary base to force our own world. Every information we recognize is created in relationship to fixed standards. In the fourth dimension, we cannot have fixed standards. When we recognize the indefinite chances in fiction or the indefinite chances in our memories, then everything is possibly executed in the present.

Heaven or Hell. Well-balanced economical creations or atom war. Right is the conclusion towards adopted standards. Wrong is everything!

Past, present, and future. Starlight the past; flower and bird the present; the black hole is the future.

The base to think is to recognize the variety of movements—movements in action and reaction that form our existence.

Dimensions mean movement in all directions at the same time. As original power for movement, we can recognize gravity. And the variation of these movements is time. The basic laws that establish most of these happenings are the contrasts or differences in movement and conditions. The power is antimatter which can produce disaster for life that sometimes can work positively or negatively.

We are in a desperate need for more correct forms of communication. The variety of the use of our language can give us knowledge. It can make us smart or intelligent. Through the broadness of word power, the number of words and understanding correctly their meanings, an educated meaning for philosophical conclusions should be formed.

Philosophy is the biggest power that guides man in his life. But the power of dimensional understanding can give man success in life and must not be ignored or misunderstood. We are obligated to bring dimensional thinking and understanding to our world of communication which may bring the power of peace to all.

The dimensions for life can be recognized in the laws of nature or movement. The power that produces movement is gravity. The power in the universe guides or controls everything through the laws it creates. The controlling part of movement on matter is time. We have the dimension of space, and with the help of communication, we form the dimension of creativity.

But life is learned in a limited way to control time. With the help of the powers of antimatter, life uses these powers to form the dimension of destruction in a controlled way—to use life to form food supply, safety or security, or quality of life. But the destiny of life is to change the movement we exist in to the existence of non-movement by the use of developed intelligence and to understand the dimension of antimatter which can form the changes. Life becomes, through the control of time, the transmission from movement we exist in to non-movement—and a beginning of a different world.

But one dimension is recognizing that the earth needs the power of gravity in its atom and molecular world which holds everything together. We need to know the dimension through forming judgment, discipline, observations, and recognitions. Intelligence, without correct knowledge, discipline, judgment, and much more, forms the power of antimatter. We have to learn that movement, the variety of movement, time, and the power of communication, build our man-made world. Imagination—our relationship to space through gravity—is one of the powers that forms our world.

Movements form units.

Man is occupied all his life with learning and
understanding the usefulness of tools.

Our knowledge about our atmosphere needs a well-observed dimensional understanding of its action and reaction. We have many questions to ask, but receive incorrect answers. What is the relationship between atmosphere and gravity? The contradicting movements in our atmosphere could bring answers when they are observed and recognized correctly.

A glider with instruments built in the aircraft can show us different responses toward the variations of different pressure changes or sound vibrations or turbulence strength or gravitational responses toward centrifugal forces created by the use of weight. We can control the inertial stability of the glider. All this can bring answers. Weight can be recognized as condensed or stored movement. Maybe sound vibrations are made visible through magnetisms, or electricity can show us the variations of atmospheric movements useful for flight.

To understand these better, we need to know the power of time and the power of movements. Gravity creates movement when it can be recognized as space power that is feeding the energies needed into the earth and to all bodies in space. That holds our atom molecular structure together.

Time is the difference of all these movements and their variety. We can recognize that time represents the transmission from movement to none or less movement, through contracts and variations.

When life is created or gets born, it learns with the help of energies to control limited time. After reaching its highest form of action, controlling the differences of movement, it slides back to non-movement and it is considered by our judgment to be dead. Life exists through its actions and performances and returns back to the dimension it came from. But through its deeds it will be remembered and will live sometimes for a long while in the world of our existence.

The universe is guided and controlled by the laws of dimensions. Life accepts these dimensions, habitually recognized in life and death, eating and drinking, sleeping or working, or to multiply for continuance of life. We learn to accept the power of antimatter as communication, contrast, discipline, and many more for a purpose to serve the needs for safety or quality living.

If we wish to become correct, we have to learn to understand time. Time is the infinite variety of the difference of movement created by the power of gravity and antimatter on everything recognizable in the dimension of creativity.

Life is related to many of these powers. It can form recognition and form judgment for quality life.

The construction of man. Imagination forms theories.
Memories and material create tools. Tools form parts.
Through transportation to assembly, all is financed by
insurance companies and banks.

The world was not built by theories—but by actions. Whatever motivates action, the meaning you put into it gives value.

Fiction, thought, and theory may build a platform for motivation. But whatever your answer is to all these questions, they will be answered according to the level of your own personal standards and evaluations.

Stop and think about it.

Our world is in a state of utter turmoil and confusion—opposing theories and opinions, wrong decision-making, poor judgment, bitter confrontations, fighting ourselves for material gain and/or influence—in order to control the world.

Our institutions which mold and guide education are outmoded the day they affect a solution. The signal changes of our time make leaders old before they get adjusted to their specific offices.

We create to fulfill the needs of our technical world of trained men. A man does not understand, but can perform by rote; men who live in a world of details with very little sense of responsibility. We create excellent education in abstract subjects and training programs, but fail to establish standards on human value.

Man promotes hidden criminals because of useful talents they possess, sometimes misused in order to gain more profit.

On what grounds can we build fair laws, financial security, and safety? The machine, the educator of modern man, teaches us three basic principles: logical thinking, good judgment, and self-discipline.

We could not start, maintain, or run a machine without "logic." We could not operate a machine and have it perform adequately without "judgment." And without "self-discipline," we would be handicapped and perhaps endangered in handling the machine. But the machine cannot give us the value or the standards we need so desperately.

I suggest that in order to handle our desperate needs for attaining value, that we form a school of philosophy to guide our educational institutions, to form and set the standards of human values that can lead us to happiness, satisfaction, and good health. I suggest an Olympic-like creative center established in the USA. I suggest we concentrate on three specific subjects:

1. *Self-evaluation* of existing talents, good or bad habits, self-criticism.

2. *Thought*—to recognize facts and their potential values before judgment-making.

3. *Self-instruction*—ninety percent of life is filled with self-instruction; i.e., learning to instruct yourself correctly.

If our future and safety depend on judgment from the majority, then we are obligated to teach men to think correctly, not good and not bad, only correctly.

To understand ourselves and the reason to be, we have to study our minds, the conscious and the unconscious, and their functions. You may say that God speaks to us through facts; to understand His words you have to use thought and recognize reality. Man does well when he lets reality control fiction. When fiction dominates reality, you will experience confusion and misery.

All of the above will be recognized and understood much more—all according to your personal standards. Just relate these precepts to your personal experiences.

We have to recognize the strongest power directing our conclusions and actions in life. It is the power of knowledge, a power that works correctly when based on collected evidence. Its side effects, common sense, logic, and facts, are well-coordinated for conclusions. In a world of movement where everything is based on laws and rules in its actions, we recognize the study of physics. Additionally we may, when we have learned to think correctly, recognize the origin, the might, and the reason to be.

In the same way we can follow the tracks of the elephants. If we study their behavior, we have a chance to find them. If we learn to follow the correct rules of physics, we may find answers to form conclusions based on collected evidence. We must recognize that thought works in all dimensions at the same time, if we are to find the origin of everything.

The greatest controversy and obstacle is untruth. We have the ability to change the roughness of the truth into a more pleasant form to accept. Lies are a power that work through emotions to form very pleasant experiences in everything before they become disasters and can ultimately end life. They are a man-made invention to create pleasant life experiences, a temporary way to form a force that can pit man against man. The strongest usually get their way.

These strong forces dominate our lives. All are dependent on our limitations. We shift from one wrong to another, completely ignoring the fundamentals, the collection of evidence. It is much easier to shift from one seemingly pleasant life to another rather than to follow the truth.

Today we are capable of rapidly collecting enormous volumes of evidence, capable of forming knowledge to force or to destroy life on earth. Failure and destruction will result in our limitations to see. We make ourselves blind to the world of the Almighty through lies that we accept as truth. The group that forms and controls lies controls the man-made world.

Man moves through life compared with a bowling ball acting on pins.

The basis for correct analysis of all existence is to understand creativity. To understand and recognize creativity, we have to recognize the laws of nature. The universe in which we live governs us by power (counter-matter), material (matter), and concurrent movements recognized in time. Creating laws is the fusion of all in the universe. Creativity begins with the highest concentration of movements overcoming obstacles with a sequence of changes that result in tangible and intangible objects. Existence is relative to products (objects) of our imagination (in creativity). Our best means of recognizing movements are engendered by imagination, which is very volatile and is independent of the visual precepts of time. They can travel to the end of our universe, as we know it, and back instantaneously.

Imagination could enable humanity to harness the energies of light for our own uses. Other intellects in the universe may have already accomplished these methods. This indicates that the universe, and we as a component thereof, are of the same origin. Our imaginative powers can travel or prospect through their confluence.

The universe exists in cycles going from minimum into action, then coming to rest. Rest means without movements (for example a black hole)—nirvana. The black hole may as well stop our imaginative powers and furnish us with wrong interpretations of falsely collected evidence, thereby keeping us uninformed about the origin of all.

The universe can be recognized by the laws of truth. Truth is conclusions formed out of collected evidence. But the black hole will eliminate our correct conclusions since it is nonexistent. How can we prove nonexistence correctly? It is the state of non-movement. For us, only movement is recognizable. The magnetic field of our earth in relationship with the electromagnetic activities in the universe furnish us with the power of imagination. Especially when we are capable of crossing these magnetic lines more often, they will supercharge us to feel great and ready for action. The evidence is furnished by a group of people enjoying the crossing of magnetic lines in motorless flight. What do they accomplish of value? Only for themselves to feel good and become unconsciously a very small part of the universe. But consciously they may experience relaxation that can help them in their daily existence. As well, they become a taste of space activities translated by the contradicting action of our atmosphere. Man ignores the laws of nature and replaces them with his own interpretation of man-made facts, dominated by religious rules or by the financial laws and with the political translations of all to serve mostly themselves. Discipline and imagination should work through as a team, and can, when understood, make life much more beautiful for all of us.

The beginning

In the realm of our existence, we can, if we wish and are blessed with an open mind, recognize the largest power in the universe. The power of antimatter. It is not a force. It represents a power. It is everywhere, in everything.

Through contrast and differences, it influences things to happen in their own way. For us, the power of antimatter becomes visible in establishing needs to invent tools for protection or to better our standards.

Mankind, wake up before you destroy yourself! Learn the use of your brain! Learn the power to recognize correctly, to evaluate your information by comparison, to form judgments or correct imaginary impulses before you act. The manner in which your brain works determines the standards of your life.

If you will be happy, satisfied, enjoy good health, and consider yourself successful, according to your personal limitations and standards, you may live a well-balanced life when you learn to stay away from extremes. As much as you may love and enjoy those extremes, they will destroy you! Our doctor bills represent the help you sought of others, which you could have handled yourself by learning in time how to use your brain. This, everybody should know!

What are we? A higher developed species of apes? Apes with brains we have never learned to use correctly? Or are we men with human qualities? Man lives by his deeds, not by the words he speaks or uses. The quality of man's deeds determines if he becomes human or remains just a man. Collect the information of our past and see how much chance we have to survive the next century, with destruction all around us and our limited control over it.

But let us start with the beginning, when man is born only by chance. Out of indefinite possibilities, you received life. Was this birth an accident, or planned by well-prepared parents? The day you begin to recognize, you will be programmed to receive information in a certain way, according to the standards adopted by your society. Existing societies adopt the same basic rules as their grandfathers before them, to make man more comfortable, both physically and mentally within these societies. Man becomes obligated to these societies, either voluntarily or through pressure from the majority. Society's rules may be different today than they were in the past and the radius of action enlarged, but the reason is still to form strong unities.

Today, strength, based on knowledge and a number of progressive tools, forms our security. According to judgment, this is not right. Our exploration of space, even setting foot on the moon, is evidence of great knowledge which becomes greater after every successful exploration. How are we using the information we gain? We use these facts to form bigger, stronger, and more mystified control systems. But how does this help man?

Man becomes more and more a living tool, programmed by memory to function when needed, but forgetting the basic rules of life. The use of the brain, in all dimensions, is not only to produce action in complicated control systems. That is, because the memory in the brain was programmed that way, it overshadows the correct use of imagination and judgment.

Our position in life is safer when we collect our information from the library and keep our own conclusions to ourselves. It would be much better if our school system would prepare students for life, and let the colleges and universities handle the specialization necessities.

Our school system has become a monster. It represents a money-grubbing institution, producing what? It calls itself an institution of education. When you possess a usable brain and you are capable of correct logic, you will find that nobody can educate you. You can be introduced to subjects, receive information or training, but you can only educate yourself.

Most teachers know the subject matter, can pass on information, and make you accept repetition and discipline, but only a few are teachers capable of guiding students out of a variety of social groups and into a fully reasoning human. As evidence, there are a great number of vandalisms and the crime rate is growing in schools. Beautiful buildings do not make good students. And successful citizens pay outrageous tax penalties for the low standard of our education and school management.

Wherever the problem is, it can be identified by the poor use of the brain of the responsible individual. We should organize and inform our educational representatives to let the right function of the brain be the guide to the students' actions. Isolate negative influences under stricter discipline and demand more production. Theoretical or physical activities are required to keep the group occupied. Poor leadership, as well as poor management, is costly, as is proven by the high taxes we have to pay. And this has all developed out of a poor schooling platform.

Man is a programmed, living computer, limited by the restricted use of memorial programming. When we turn back information about history, we find that the collection of our recordings is only relatively useful. Most recordings are the answer to man's action dominated by a group of the strong. The winner will tell the historian what he has to accept and record as truth. Other information is destroyed, including the historian who could bring harm to strong organizations with his recordings.

If we turn history further back, we find that the earth was in the process of constant changes, meteorological or geophysical, which brought man to need. To compensate for his necessities, he formed groups in order to forcefully fulfill his needs from others. Sometimes this was successful; sometimes it was disastrous, and an existence of horror and fear was created. Man was witted against man using incomparable methods of brutality, sadism, and cruelty in order to fulfill his demands. To become stronger, man invented philosophies, some of which were based on promises, some on riches and hope, and some on faith. He organized groups held together by these philosophies and favor. Their leader became king physically, but philosophically he made himself a god and was worshiped as such. Their ruling forces were fear and favors; their tools hearsay, corruption, flat untruth, and mystery or magic to fool the majority. These philosophies became religious and only the strong religions survived. Some became so strong that they became rulers, and kings became puppets. God became more and more earthly and the rules became very practical so as to serve man in his greed.

This has not yet changed. Only God has become more distant, a personified mystery, but still with human limitations. Today God is a myth of man, with almighty powers and able to do everything according to man's imagination and the standards of the worshiper. But while religious forces collided, a gained sense of exploration and adventure grew. A very strong force could develop: the force of knowledge. This force could be used for destruction as well as for administration and rebuilding. Knowledge has created tools and these tools have opened up the world to facts and a wisely controlled combination of forces and laws. More and more the mystery of happenings has been lost in favor of well-functioning man. Man is using these forces of knowledge for his protection. But when man is still controlled by man-made gods, where does all this lead us?

Who created the laws that enable everything to function correctly? You may recognize that God or a creative force or a superior being uses these laws to communicate to the intellect. In other words facts represent the words of God to all! But all cannot recognize facts. Yet we make the rulers of our faith, who with their votes cast the strong leaders into office.

We possess the tools to destroy this living world, but we lack the forces to govern these tools safely. All falls back on one conclusion: the correct use of our brain is and has been neglected. A profusion of languages makes it almost impossible to communicate accurately. Our schooling serves to feed hungry businesses with trained brains and it pays millions of trainers their wages. Our schools use limited, wrong philosophies to feed the masses with mind-destructive under-attainment. Religious organizations represent billions of dollars in operations, so their God is a businessman rather than a God of mercy, love, and faith. Who tells us this? God, Himself, by using facts to warn us. But if He wishes to destroy us, He will give us blindness and we will destroy ourselves. A very dangerous form of existence! The right philosophy, the theory of our existence, cause and reason has to be utilized as a guide to our growing knowledge. And conclusions have to be based on facts: the word of God.

If you wish to be correct, you have to learn to be truthful; truthful to yourself by evaluating your personal experiences correctly. Be careful in using another man's conclusions without rechecking their value on truthfulness, recognize your limitations, and altogether form your standards. What guides man's actions? How does man collect his information and put it to use? Man's senses recognize; man's brain collects the recognized information; and by comparison he evaluates its importance. The stored information, through memory, can be reproduced by the individual when desired.

What motivates man to action? Man possesses three memories: the memory of the conscious mind, the memory of the unconscious mind, and the inherent memory. The inherent memory controls your talents, your physical appearance, and so on. The unconscious mind is your motor mind and controls your heartbeat and other body functions in a mixed functioning of all minds together. But all have connecting parts and are changed by the constant changes of our gravity, electromagnetic, and outer space forces. These changes activate our fictional or imaginary parts and forms, experienced and guided by judgment, into motivating our actions. Judgmental talents are based on the gift to recognize differences and compare their value for a purpose. The purpose is to guide information into usable creations to protect man or satisfy his personal standards.

To guide and control these indefinite experiences, man formed his theories to guide his knowledge into carefully fitted or loosely thrown together conclusions. Generally, this is accepted as philosophy. Philosophy is the force that guides our knowledge in a constructive form, which should be accepted by all men on earth, independent of physical or educational differences.

What has formed our knowledge? Some men have the talent to form useful tools out of their collected information. These tools are described and their functions explained and collected in books, libraries, or on film. But the correct use of these tools must be guided by the right philosophy. Otherwise knowledge may be as dangerous as a loaded gun in the hands of a monkey.

The amount of our knowledge can be measured by the understanding of tools we have learned to master and to put to use. If we use the right philosophy to guide us in our logical recognition, this knowledge can lead us in a world of beauty and happiness, and keep us satisfied. It will be a reality; what is today only a dream in many men's minds.

Our biggest enemy is generally called stupidity. Stupidity is the limited use of the brain or its function, limited by ignorance, laziness, physical handicaps, inheritance, etc. Most unpleasant experiences are formed from stupidity. Many office holders do not have the level of brain activity required to meet the responsibility of the office held. Mostly based on judgment, practiced without evidence or only partially correct information, short temper or stubbornness, forms a tool for poor judgment. The importance of clearing the understanding of stupidity becomes a necessity. We have to recognize the importance of fairness as well. Fairness is the measuring stick for one's deeds. We will be judged by the standards of our own demonstrated philosophy. Man is not equal; his deeds determine his standards. Man does not live by theories or words alone, he lives by his executed deeds. When man is judged by other philosophies, he will mostly become radical and accept severe penalties before he will change his ideologies.

The rules of existence are based on strength. The majority gives strength, but makes nothing right. We do not possess the knowledge to be absolutely right. What we possess is the knowledge to reason and that can make wrong more right and less wrong. But the handicap lies in that only a few have the gift for progressive reasoning. What we know of reasoning survives to win judgment out of selfish motivations.

But that will become the past. We have the knowledge and are capable of collecting information that will guide us in a new world of harmony among men. When not, we have only a short time until some man will make a mistake, influenced by man-made religions, uncontrollable rays from outer space, or poorly controlled brain action. Whatever it is, we may experience what is hard to express in words. Let me show you that this can be the beginning of a better world of beauty toward man and beast.

We have to recognize that knowledge is a collection of information, collected through evidence or verbal translation plus imagination. Additionally we have to understand that our knowledge-collective mind works mainly through emotions, intelligence, or common sense. A mixture of all is mostly practiced. First, we have to learn to control our emotions. Second, we have to know what intelligence is. Intelligence is the collection of information in the broad sense, mixed with well-functioning memories for reproduction and mixture. Mostly we are very lenient in acceptance of accuracy in favor of being understood or easy to use and impressive. We have many instructors, teachers, and trainers passing on regulations for emotions and intelligence. Third is the art of understanding the value of common sense. Common sense represents the effort used to be correct in everything and every time. Man created for his safety and progress tools for almost everything, tools for communication, transportation, movement in three dimensions, and so on. The most brilliant men created or invented the tools by disciplining their imaginations into, for us, useful creations. Imagination is the greatest power to motivate our existence. To use these tools correctly we have to learn to discipline ourselves to understand and use these tools to the best of their performance. That is common sense.

The most important figure in all betting organizations is the loser.
He pays for everything.

What formed the laws of existence and reason? It could be the main force to study in order to find better answers for man's behavior. Man is a creation of many energies on elements according to conditions and changes on earth, an ironical creation, the product of the indefinite possibilities in space, or a carefully planned creation by forces still logically unknown to us. But these can become reality in each of us by imaginary conclusions. Let us start to explore our world from that angle of view. There are only a few unpleasant experiences in our existence. They all could be handled when recognized in time, when we can expose our brain actions or cure fear in other extremes, and help detect diseases or sickness so they can be treated in time.

But all can only be turned into a realization when we learn to accept the right philosophy and base the conclusions on facts: the word of God. When you understand that you must study harder and learn to meditate correctly, you will recognize the wisdom of God in everything. We have to learn to live correctly right from the beginning, not live and depend on help from others, or when we find out we get hurt by enjoying the extremes too much. Extremes are destructive, and we need a strong control based again on constructive philosophy, not on emotional impulses or imaginary conclusions, but on facts: the words of the Almighty.

Organized imagination, with the help of energy formed everything man has created. Flight is the most dynamic example of our current state in time. More exotic forms must follow.

We live in an era of rapidly expanding knowledge, and with the advent of electronically operated Computers, we can obtain stereotyped solutions to many defined problems. We are prone to allow our gadgetry to direct our lives in mundane ways that inhibit originality and exploration of other concepts. In the process we tend to lose our initiative. We find it less and less appealing to think and pursue new avenues of theory. Our computerized habit has caused us to rely on "stored" information, or in effect, to "live in the past," and we think in retrospect rather than by projections based on newly developed facts or hypotheses. We bask in the comfort of mental stagnation, wanting to ignore that to exist is to be continually in motion, and that we cannot tolerate a static condition for long.

When confronted with our daily problems, we find it much easier to rely on the printed words of others who are many times merely self-appointed "experts" in a given field. We may subjugate ourselves to "media solutions" that we are bombarded daily by television and radio. There is a subtle premium paid for this comfortable, unimaginative existence. We lose our individuality and freedom. We become programmed drones controlled by an intangible minority operating through convenient, sacrosanct devices that, in effect, direct our thoughts and actions in every phase of our lives. We subject ourselves to a fear complex and become as cattle who only respond to mental and physical threats. We fear loss of our physical possessions, so we rely on media imposed solutions that only result in other problems. We allow ourselves to apply centralized solutions to our own particular situations and thereby never solve our own particular needs. We pawn our individuality for temporary and convenient relief as professed by others.

We cannot continue for long to rely on the "solutions" of others. We have the tools available to break out of our stagnation, if we will only acknowledge and apply them as our previous and incidentally more progressive societies did.

We need to rediscover art, all forms of it, but mostly in paintings because they are static and can be observed continually. Art is a visual presentation of the thinking process. Each painting should carry a central theme or message for the uninhibited mind.

In the quiet recesses of an art gallery, we can observe true art. In sound, art can be expressed through poetry, music, or subjects introduced and discussed with the general public. In paintings and sculptures, the true meaning of the laws of nature or the word of God should not be neglected. They will begin to oven up our minds to new thoughts and speculations.

Even the oldest works of the oldest masters can speak to our so-called modern minds if we will allow them, whether through the brutal cubism of a recent Picasso or the subtler forms and colors of others, such as Millet, Gaugin, Monet, and Van Gogh.

Essentially graphic art exists in the eyes of the beholder and cannot exist through the eyes of others. It is immune to computerized pro-gramming and keypunched solutions. We insist on pure water for our good physical health, yet we accept all kinds of liquid pollution for our mental health. Art is like cool water from a remote mountain spring, coming to us in a pure form, direct to the window of our mind. It can be expected to result in pure and uncontaminated thought. Artists often comment on how little children, with yet comparatively pure minds, can Comprehend the meanings of their paintings more readily than their parents or elders.

Man's greatest possession is good health, both physical and mental. Man has also refused to realize that these are profoundly related. Art is a pure food for mental health and concomitantly for physical well-being. We should take our minds back to the beginnings and rediscover the universal truths expressed in good analysis followed by correct action. What better way to exercise the mind under uncontaminated conditions? Watching others perform on a TV set in the comfort of our own homes is an unacceptable mental and physical placebo that is destroying the minds and bodies of all of us. Individualism is becoming a state to be avoided in the eyes of the masses.

To break the pall of mediocrity, we need to seek our freedom from mental, moral, and physical programmed servitude, and what better way than that which has been suggested? We must again dare to be individuals and accent any temporary penalties. True, few will have the mettle to pursue new and maybe maverick oaths to the potential rewards of excellence, but is has always been "the way of all flesh" that purity in thought and action will triumph and lead the way for the few out of desperation and futility. Time, the ultimate controlling force and universal discipline, will demand it to be so.

Life formed man with the help of the laws of nature to a master of creativity. Through electromagnetic fields and the flow of electrons and chemical chances of matter into energy, man learned to store information (memories). He learned to establish the power for judgment. Man exists in time, represented in the variety of objects to show confusion in his existence. Man has to learn to discipline and organize with the help of laws. The books represent memories. The drawings show theories. The basic shades are the performed creativities on objects. The chemical process for energies. the base for creativity, is represented in food, oxygen, liquid, and electromagnetic impulses and particles all over the canvas. Man's destiny is repetition, imitation, and destruction to exist, expressed in the parrot and turkey. The rest is up to the observer—to collect suggestive information to form his personal standards among man to form his life.

Time is the contrasting movements on the difference of matter—or gravity is movement; time is the difference and forms the infinite creations in matter.

Time is the difference of movements. Everything that exists and is measurable and can be detected is a trace of matter in a state of movement, and the difference of these movements in time. The contrasting differences of these movements can be measured by comparison with each other. It is counter-matter on matter.

We have to recognize that movement can go in seven dimensions at the same time. It can, by understanding it correctly, be a process of thought. But most of the time a part of the dimensions is used, and we are all full of errors when we reach conclusions.

Life is a creation of matter and counter-matter in a state of indefinite movements (or time). Life receives the right to play with time when created in the beginning, with help, and later it becomes more and more independent. That can mean that life can go unlimited into action in all directions at the same time. Life becomes capable of speeding or slowing down and changing time in its movement. That is our destiny. When our existence changes, what we call death, we return to matter and counter-matter but lose the right to play with time. That is the law of our existence and it becomes understandable when we can recognize that every cell in our body is an independent self-moving creation that functions in group movement for accomplishments. And all together this forms us into what we are.

We will learn to understand these better when we use artwork to communicate with each other and to try to be correct in our collection of information and conclusions. Scientists communicate through pictures, but this is not called art or accepted as art—just blueprints. But this form of communication is much more correct than sound or its interpretations because it is based on accepted standards. Meaning in art can produce the best form of education to all.

What is art? Life is protected and guided by the acceptance of standards. The dimensional broadness of these standards can give us happiness, good health, and satisfaction. When these statements are molded to the changes in time, artwork can play an important role in doing so.

We can observe that all life accepts standards. It is a necessity for survival and it becomes habitable to life. We can find that as more brain is available, then more standards are accepted by the species. Man developed numerous forms of standardization. This includes man's acceptance of rules in physics and mathematical conclusions. It is a compromise to understand the world our way. The world is movement in all direction at the same time, not measurable with our tools and above our thinking power. Artwork should be a creation of a team. These covers display which should motivate man's thoughts to recognize the forms of action. Action that creates beauty and meanings in all forms of display, a real form that creates power.

An artist by himself cannot produce art. He is influenced by his limitation to interpret his personal experiences and impressions. The absolute freedom of expression can go positive or negative. Positive needs organized acceptance of life. Negative is an explosion of confusion, emotionally experienced and expressed on a level of cannibalism and rape to serve the artist's personal desires without responsibilities toward mankind.

Artwork consists of many things that can only be produced by a team. It consists of the science of philosophic origin. We need financial Dower and the multi-craftsmanship in the execution. It should represent a good interpretation of existing values or suggest better existing standards. Observers have to learn to be motivated to accept better forms of life for themselves and for their relationships with others. We have to recognize the powers through organized values, forms, shades, and color combinations that produce creations of art. But all together it is movement and the difference of infinite forms of action—or movement is time.

We live in a world guided by knowledge based on accepted standards. The acceptance of a correct philosophy is a must to guide and control our actions. Knowledge without correct Philosophy is a must to guide and control our actions. Knowledge without correct philosophy is dangerous like a loaded gun in the hands of monkeys.

Rails represent guidance for railroad cars for better performance to transportation—weight times distance with the least use of energies. Schools are rails for man to better his productions. They discipline and help his performance. Man has to learn to serve the demands of his communities.

In the realm of our existence, we can, if we wish and are blessed with an open mind, recognize the largest power in the universe; the power of antimatter. It is not a force. It represents a power. It is every-where, in Everything. Through contrast and differences, it influences things to happen in its own way. For us, it becomes visible in establishing needs in us to invent tools for protection or to better our standards.

The need for religion and absolute authority, to recognize a soul, demands a form of movement in all directions—a process of develop-ment very little developed with the guidance of man. It was and is a reaction toward energies in constant change by chemo, chemo-electric, magnetic, gravity, inertia, and many other acting forces. Sometimes it is guided by instinct, need, more or less exposure toward happenings, but mostly it is exposed by the laws of chance—constantly gaining speed or movement in all directions by the use of tools that give us movement—through recognizing, concluding, and executing the final force that gives speed necessary to free matter and the cycle is closed.

Through repeated reading and study of sided effects of thought splinters, we can form condensed logical conclusions through the power of repetition that our universe exists in a bubble of gravity. Everything is related to or affected by gravity. No light can shine or be recognized as such without gravity. No magnetism can exist. The flow of electricity could not form or act without gravity. And our imaginations would not work at all.

Black holes are difficult to observe because they stop light. The attracting powers in the black hole absorb gravity and light cannot be observed. Our universe is created out of atoms, molecules, and energies related to matter. They need energy to hold together for billions of years. They receive energy through gravity.

Our physical existence needs energies as well in order to hold together. Gravity passes through us into the earth, leaving us with the impression that the earth is pulling us. This is expressed in weight and translated as condensed movement in percentage. Our atmosphere is filled with moisture, dust particles, and different gases so that gravity can be filled with solar energies which form solar storms and other activities in the universe. This form changes very slowly to be recognized as compared with the fast but short time of our life or existence.

Life can change movement into time by contradiction of infinite forms of movement into time or contradiction of movements on the difference of matter. In the process it forms creativity. We can observe and recognize this in the variety of living creations surrounding our existence. This will happen after man has learned to meditate correctly and to pray for wisdom and the art to see not only with his eyes but with all of his being.

The base of the immutable, cosmic law rests on chance as on the roll of the die. Of all entities, only animals and men have the power of choice— the red, green, or yellow apple. But only man has the Dower of reason, which he must learn to use—as in a game of chess or on the battlefront.

CREATIVITY BY MAN.

SMARTNESS is a gift of inheritance.

INTELLIGENCE can be reached through schooling.

COMMON SENSE is a product of experience.

But few are lucky and have a little of all.

Part 2

What is Gravity?
How Does It Appear To Work?

We may recognize through gravity the strongest source of power. It brings location changes to matter. We can observe a variety of changes in the electromagnetic fields and solar storms and others to form the movements in our universe. Each object that is constructed by the atom or molecular movement forms a vacuum for space energies. These need to be recharged to replace the energies used to keep things together and needed to produce its own variety of matter.

On earth we have life, water, atmosphere, and a variety of chemical processes. They all need energies. Some can be produced by the planet itself, but all cannot be produced by the planet alone and this forms a vacuum toward the universe.

Space, with all its excesses of all kinds, forms fundamental energies. We exist under an influence of steady pressure moving toward the most energy-using part of the earth. The iron magnetic ring creating the electricity for movement in our atoms and molecular structure produces as well the magnetism needed to keep the moon in orbit and to hold our own position in the solar system.

Life is protected by the atmosphere which filters the space energies to a bearable form and amount for life. But we can observe that life is often destroyed by too much exposure to space energies. Everything has to be in balance. Quick changes can bring disaster. When exposed to life, life has to change, move, or die.

We may assume that gravity is not a pulling power but a vacuum. It is created by the need to form and find the sources of energies which hold the electron structure in the atom and the molecular assembly together. To create the needs for life and life's power for functioning, it may be the power of the universe or a part of it. Penetrating flows in the direction of the earth's center or its energy-forming and changing iron-rich ring surrounding the earth's center form the earth's magnetic field.

According to Newton, a feather and steel will travel at the same speed in a vacuum when exposed to gravity. But when they become stationary they will receive weight according to their molecular density. But in outer space we have weightlessness and all will move according to their inertia to different rules of physics. There must be something incorrect in the Newton Theories. What is the difference when an object is pulled or pushed or moves with the stream of its surroundings? The answer: Where does the energy come from? How strong is it? And how long will it last? Or how well is it used for intellect to create? Man moves with the help of gravity. We move in flight and many other creations through gravity.

Each object forms a vacuum. Planets, fix stars, and smaller objects for space energies are limited by size, density, heat movements, magnetisms, atomic energies, production, and energies output. When the space energies meet the influence of the energy vacuum absorbing objects, then all objects will continue at the same speed. But when they become stationary they will be exposed in their atoms and molecular structure to the vacuum of the planet and that forms weight. That means they have to absorb the energies to stay together in the molecular structure they exist in. And that means weight.

In space we experience weightlessness when the distance is farther than the power of the vacuum, but our solar system exists in a pressure pool of space energies. Two larger objects close to each other producing energy vacuums will create an energy shortage between the two. That means weight for stationary objects and the earth's centrifugal forces can lift some of the earth's surface, recognizable as high and low tides.

If Newton were correct, we would have changes in weather every eight hours. Atmosphere has weight and would be effected by the moon's gravity with the water. But I am convinced that gravity is created and produced in the universe with similar effects that keep us guessing. We believe that the moon lift's our earth's surface, well recognizable as high and low tides, but it has little recognizable effect on our atmosphere. But atmosphere represents weight, recognizable in the indicated variations on our barometers which would be effected by the strength of the moon.

When we are exposed to space pressure changes, then centrifugal force will lift the earth's surfaces, but this would have very little influence on changes in our atmosphere. When we become capable of recognizing that we exist in a pool of space energies only disturbed by the difference of energy needs of surrounding objects, we may recognize the powers that create gravity.

To understand gravity better, we have to learn to recognize the power of time. Time equals the contrasting movements on the difference of matter. The variety of space energies filtered by time is a variety of creation. We are part of it. Let us observe infinite parts we consist of and learn to understand the functioning. We may become confused by the variety of actions and responses. For centuries we existed, guided through wrong conclusions and poor judgments that form limitations, and we unconsciously hurt ourselves and others.

It would be interesting to study the reason for life in the universe. To my conclusion, life is capable of creating and forming intellect. That means, according to its findings, interpretations, collections, translations, experiences, and many more, life forms its own creativity. But it can as well create its own destruction to exist. When we become capable of recognizing the cycles in the universe, we will find that existence to nonexistence is a cycle. We may assume that movement is existence and non-movement is nonexistence.

Evidence for movement is our existence and the extension of the universe. Evidence for non-movement is that we know so very little about the black hole, a great concentration of space energies in a relatively small area. Undetectable information—it is no existing. Life is capable of creating the changes from movement to non-movement, creating the beginning of a black hole or forming the beginning of a black hole as part of a rebirth in the universe.

This was filmed in February 1987: Two circling fixed stars around a non-visible center were observed. After a length of time the outline of a third star became visible. Or the third star was a black hole full of space energies. The fixed stars brought movement into the black hole. It became visible and the power in the following explosion had never been observed before. It formed a new part of the universe. The cycle was closed. Life could have had a part in it. And it gives life an important part in the existence of the universe.

****

Let us recognize out of the summation of thought splinters our dimensional existence. Dimensional existence, used with correct discipline, can form a universal philosophy to peacefully unify man. Thereafter man can make fascinating discoveries in space and ocean exploration to benefit our world, creating a pleasant lifestyle for all.

We must recognize that life is controlled by basic principles. Our life is controlled:

1. by gravity. Gravity gives us movement in all directions.
    We can learn to control gravity through discipline;

2. by the use of time. Time is the variation of difference on
    matter. Life learns how to use time through the difference
    of memory processes;

3. by contrasting powers. Day and night, hot and cold, wet and dry, contrasting powers build creation. Life on earth could not have been produced if not for these pavers. Contrasting forces develop antimatter, the power of creativity;

4. by learning to control space through creative linear thinking. We can recognize In our surroundings items like the location of power and pipe lines, the laying of railroad lines and streets. Our language is linear, used to give linear directions for orientation. The above examples would not become true otherwise;

5. by the use of destruction to support life or to elevate the quality of life. We harvest crops for food and utilize natural resources for building material;

6. by the destruction of change resulting from halting the motion of gravity through use of negative temperature. Movement is formed by gravity resulting in heat. Only movement is recognizable. Non-movement is hard to detect. With temperatures less than 273 degrees Celsius, movement can be stopped, forming a black hole.

The universal power of gravity forms movement. It is a part of every form of existence. Light travels on gravity and without it, sunlight could not shine. We likewise would not have electricity or magnetism. Both of these energies depend on movement related to gravity.

We exist In dimensions. That means movement can work in all directions at the same time. But man created his own interpretation to understand the world from a stationary, or limited, prospective. Our stationary angle, expressed in physics, mathematics, and chemistry, creates a contradiction.

When it comes to dimensional existence, we make the dimensional appear stationary by explaining new discoveries with theories. For example gravity, light, contrasting powers, and time are dimensional powers but are only understood by man when explained as stationary. When it can be made understandable that light travels on the power of gravity, then many of the existing scientific rules and theories will have to change.

We must recognize the powers of bacterial actions to assist or destroy our living conditions In order to exist. This has direct Influence on the formation of Judgment.

Life can be recognized with different values. People are Judged as well-educated, intellects, smart, and well-disciplined. Also we have the limited brain users, deemed stupid, because of incorrect judgment to gain profit. They misuse their confidence to hurt others out of selfish reasons.

Considering all of the above suggestions, correct judgment is the most Important asset to man. We can develop our own personal quality of judgment by using tools to form controversy. We must learn to judge correctly all experiences to produce values usable to all.

I suggest that a glider should be used as one tool. Gliders produce three-dimensional controversies which can only be successfully controlled with correct judgment. Flight safety consists of proper judgment of the pilot on the ground and in the three-dimensional framework of the air with his aircraft in use.

With the frequent use of gliders, we can develop correct use of judgment for all life experiences, not just in the air.

When exposed to different, contradicting experiences, we can make a wide variety of decisions. But what is the best decision, for what reason, and in what time? The variables are endless. We must therefore consider that all things are related to gravity, time, and space, and can be guided through proper judgment.

Time

Time, the ultimate medium of existence, is a function of the seven dimensions that compose it, as will be explained in the treatise that follows. Expression in the scientific community has reached an impasse via the integration of mathematics. The thought vectors of advanced mathematics are a limited means of communication, bringing us to only four of the seven dimensions, the last of which is termination or non-matter. Transit to the seventh dimension seeks other forms of expression to be understood and hence is exploited by mankind. The exponential capacity of art has been virtually ignored as an adjunct to expanded communication.

Art, the universal expression, is not limited by linguistic declensions or mathematical symbols and theorems. It offers a purity that is not hindered by emotion or religious dogma, readily comprehended by the yet simplistic mind of a child. Before further progress in understanding time and its composition of contracts, we must adopt a new communication means which will permit a greater interchange of thought vectors or ideas. It follows that a seven-dimensional approach, vice four, will offer limitless possibilities and can only be realized with other means of communication.

In a time when we are exploring space and floating objects in the sky, we also should be exploring the powers that create everything.

Gravity and time can be the powers that furnish us with the information we need to recognize the power, not the forces. Gravity produces the power of action while time creates the variety of existing forms, shapes, objects, and conditions.

We have to learn to understand through a correct philosophy of ourselves. Additionally, we have to study the reasons for being. We need a different approach to recognize the correct philosophy and the basic powers that form and create everything. For life, this means the power that forms creativity. It consists of imagination, judgment, communication, memory, and more. It consists of a mixture of anti-matter and matter in a constant form of movement which brings all the changes to matter created by man.

We exist in a world of movement—a mixture of atoms and molecules energized by a flow of electrons. Groups of living cells form into bodies to function as representatives of living creatures. Nothing known so far exists in a single form. We exist in dimensions. Artwork can explain the dimensional form we exist in. It consists in powers of communication, memories, emotional influences, greed, mixed with judgment in all forms of action.

We exist in dimensions. The first dimension is movement. Gravity and other forces produce the action. The second dimension is time that forms the contrasting movement on matter. The third dimension is space. The fourth dimension forms communication judgment or is the dimension of antimatter. The fifth dimension forms the power of creativity, from a splinter of thought to a product with the help of energies, and forms accomplishments. The sixth dimension is life. The seventh dimension forms changes or destruction.

With the power of time we can recognize time as transmission from non-movement to movement in our form of existence. We can recognize a relationship between gravity and imagination. We can recognize gravity through weight. Many mechanical creations made by man are a combination of weight's use on each other. Time is formed or created through movements, but time cannot create movement.

We can observe that all mechanical creations or mechanical accomplishments are based on written information or drawings for communication and accuracy. They appear in three dimensions. The explanations serve for the communication that represents the fourth dimension. We exist in several recognized dimensions, but our conclusions are only correct to man's judgment. We know very little about time, gravity, imagination, judgment, and more. That is all created in time.

Man is guided by his own philosophy to act. His philosophy is based most strongly on his personal experience or on judgment from people he trusts most. A great part of our philosophical conclusions are based on faith, beliefs, or habits.

When man is growing up, he learns fast that philosophies cannot be trusted, so he forms a workable philosophy out of his own experiences. When we can learn to understand the powers of gravity and time, we may discover a powerful and dependable philosophy that could help all people face their problems successfully. They will recognize that political solutions rather than philosophies create the problems on earth. They form the power for leading people to support special groups out of selfish reasons.

Powers and Principles

If we wish to communicate with the powers of nature or with God, we have to learn to understand principles. God communicates to all forms of life through the power of principles.

From interpretations of principles, we formulate details. The simplest example of a principle and detail can be the necessity for a person to travel from Dallas to New York City. The need for travel is the principle. To travel by aircraft, ship, automobile, bicycle, or on foot is the detail.

We live and are controlled by man-made details. The result, however, brings us into a vast amount of controversy. With the freedom of interpretation and judgment, we enlarge differences between opinion, culture, etc., creating the controversy—all through the use of emotion and false securities. We create unfairness and judge translations of experience by the use of changing details.

Education is a principle. We can develop the power for correctly using it. Education is the sum of experience, and through proper deeds and truthfully spoken words, we can demonstrate our educational standards. But what are we doing? We are using the educational system to progress our own personal definition of civilization. Unfortunately at the same time we are neglecting to advance our philosophy to a higher level to properly guide our deeds and actions. History shows that people who have never had a formal education prove to be better educated than many university students graduating with degrees and honors but who later turn to crime and other negative actions. These educated people are violating the law to hurt people out of greed or selfish reasons.

When we believe that schools and training can educate man, then what does the entertainment world teach us? The principles of entertainment teach us every form of crime and negative form of action, perpetuating the hurting and killing of others. Again actions conducted for selfish reasons. Within the process of crime, witnesses are destroyed so that no evidence is left for traceability. With regret, we have too much evidence in the real world that people conduct and get away with these actions. Hence it can be said that the entertainment world has negative input to the social behavior of our communities.

For us to progress, we must form an acceptable philosophy that will be correct for all. We must develop a philosophy that will give the least amount of controversy or difference. Let us use imagination as the product of collecting correct evidence to form a well-functioning judgment, creating a philosophy for guiding life and action. With luck, we can learn the correct use of knowledge even when crime might represent the easiest way to get power, money, and other valuables.

Our new guiding philosophy should be treated as a science. Men of vast differences in background and culture accept without question the benefits of modern transportation. Other practices globally accepted are the advancement of medicine and agriculture. Such should be the approval of our new philosophy—acceptance based on logical benefits. When we can teach man to accept the right form of principles, the creation of movement such as gravity and the powers of creativity in the form of time, we can establish a well-functioning philosophy where mankind can solve his problems and obtain his goals of safe living.

We have to understand education to establish a successful life for man. Education consists of a well-disciplined and organized form of imagination and judgment. It has to be based on a fair exchange of action. No one can educate anyone. You can only educate yourself through the use of disciplined judgment mixed with well-organized imagination—the power that creates everything accomplished by man.

Everything exists in a state of movement. Types of matter and energies have been discovered to be smaller than atoms and lower than electrons. The combination of these elements form molecules, the basic building blocks of our universe.

Technology is continuously being advanced to enhance our quality of life. Unfortunately our philosophical developments lag far behind. We continue to use philosophies based on three to four thousand-year-old theories, keeping us misinformed about ourselves and our neighbors.

We live in a world of movement in all directions at the same time. For most of mankind, only a limited amount is successfully used and only very little is understood.

Wake up, mankind. Accept the correct laws of nature. Elevate your standards in life. We consist of spiritual powers related to space. These spiritual powers discovered the right conditions on earth and a good reason to create life in the form of living cells. These cells developed a process of multiplication to form, through creativity, life in all forms of senses to shape existing conditions through the use of contrasting powers—such as dark and light, hot and cold, wet and dry—and differences in pressure changes and many more things. These all create the fundamental powers to create or form life.

A combination of cells is combined in infinite structures to create what we find today. Every movement is done by a group of cells with different functioning and controlled by spiritual influences. Specially developed cells which are stored in groups, along with the help of magnetism and electricity, function as the brain. This is done through imagination and judgment, influenced through space and through the use of collected experiences to form recognition in time.

To understand spiritual powers, man has to learn to accept the fact that all that exists in dimensions is created through movement and time. Let us explore the power of a language. We learn and memorize sound waves, invent signs to make sound visible, and form spiritual meanings into relative stationary reality.

Religion is expressed through individualism, expressed and understood to man's personal standards through man's imagination and judgment. It becomes a private affair.

I challenge YOU, "Wake up, mankind." It is time to accept the correct laws of nature.

To develop a successful life for man, we must understand education correctly. Today's fiction, controlled by man-made laws, rules, and beliefs, may be tomorrow's reality.

Thought splinters can become correct when it is understood that conclusions were formed from guidance through gravity, time, space, communication, and other things.

All movements on earth are related to gravity. A big gravity bubble in the universe furnished the power controlling our solar system and through movement forms contrast such as light and dark, hot and cold, wet and dry, and many more contrasting appearances.

It is this base that forms life and everything—because we exist in a world of movement. There is no movement at a temperature of minus 276 degrees Celsius—no movement can develop. Movement represents temperature and we can detect temperature in every movement.

Now start the movements necessary in your own system of cells to recognize what is reality, not the imagination of others. Just learn to think, not to repeat. Evaluate information as the foundation of your personal success.

To develop a successful life for man, we must use education logically. True education consists of a well—disciplined and organized form of imagination and judgment. It has to be based on a fair exchange of action. No one can educate anyone. You can only educate yourself through the use of disciplined judgment mixed with well organized imagination—the power that creates all accomplishments by mankind.

A fundamental principle to help guide education is the creative process of movement. God and the powers of nature communicate to all through principles of movement. As we know, everything exists in a state of movement. Gravity is the force that drives movement and time creates the difference in existence, giving form, shape, and condition. Scientists have discovered matter smaller than atoms and energies lower than electrons, all of which are in motion. The combination of the infinitesimal elements builds molecules. Molecules hold our universe together and make us what we are.

To communicate with these powers of creativity, we must learn to divide principles from details. We live, however, in a world dominated by man-made interpretations of principles. A school, for example, represents a detail. It is a detail to train people the understanding of man-made creations.

We believe that schools are needed to achieve a successful and profitable life. But what education standard does the entertainment world give us? Entertainment in the form of television and movies shows us a world of crime and all negative actions in our society. What is particularly harmful is that it is becoming increasingly accessible to children. It has been said before that a picture is worth more than a thousand words. Think how dangerous that is. School teaches us how to make a living and entertainment teaches us crime, both geared toward making money.

Schools can likewise teach rocket science, but what spiritual value have we gained by setting foot on the moon? We indeed gained knowledge, but knowledge without philosophy is dangerous and can lead to self-destruction. A classic example is man's ability to apply knowledge toward, waging war. Where are the philosophical strengths based on the discipline of the Ten Commandments, fairness among men, and self-control. The lack of control we see today has given us overpopulation and over-production of weapons. Both destructive to mankind. Based on monetary income, schools teach science for the creation of destructive merchandise, all being controlled by the majority—the limited brain users.

With our misunderstanding of education, what does the future have in store for us?

Dear Reader:

Why is man capable of setting foot on the moon or adventuring in space?

Because scientists have a more accurate form of communicating with each other to create reality. But the general public communicates by sound. We form words and sentences to make ourselves understood by using the different variations of sound waves. In the process of thought, as well as by reading, we are using imagination, a silent form of sound to communicate with ourselves.

But let us use vision, a more correct form of communication than sound, to make us understood! How often do we experience the use of beautiful sounding words saying very little and plain language saying a lot. Take the approach of these pictures as a suggestion to deal with the problem. Use the blessing you received from life, skill, and talent, and express your knowledge, ideas, and thoughts on canvas or sculpture to create the conversation or argument of the artist. How should a scientist differ from the artist? Only by the form of communication!

Hans Tormolen

TO RECOGNIZE TIME BETTER, A LATE THOUGHT SPLINTER

Everything that exists has its past, present, and future. It comes and goes and works in cycles—some it short, repeating changes; some may take many years before producing a cycle. But it is time that creates, forms, and brings changes to matter, brings differences to everything. The great creative power that is formed through different laws makes the variety for self-creation.

EPILOGUE

To support our authorities and to help them protect and guide us to quality life, we are obligated to set our philosophical standards based on scientific knowledge formed on the collection of evidence and logic.

Life was given to us through the powers of matter, space, movement (in the form of gravity), and time (the power of creativity). Time forms judgment, which is the power of antimatter.

Life, when born or created, receives the power of time.

Life learns to understand and to use time. To control time, life uses memories. After life learns to store and reproduce information when desired, a mixture of all forms of stored information, remembered and reproduced, is mostly considered a thinking process. We have to learn to consider that we possess two minds: the conscious and the unconscious.

The conscious mind represents a collection of memories. The unconscious mind represents a power energized directly by energies; like oxygen that we breathe through lungs and skin. We eat and drink to produce temperature and molecule changes. We are directly influenced through time in our unconscious actions. We can control our conscious mind through correct meditation. But we can contact the dimensional power of time through our unconscious mind, through information and our self-control.

Another form that threatens our quality of life is the misuse of the freedom of tongue and action. To honor the freedom established by a nation and which we enjoy, we are obligated to serve with understanding the necessity of discipline and self-control.

Freedom of tongue and uncontrolled action forms controversy, fanatics, and radicals—the power that creates every unpleasant form of life we go through.

With the help of our imagination, the formation of judgment through our five senses recognized through the power of space, movement or gravity, matter, and time, we are related to the universe.

With our physical existence after death, we go back to matter. After losing more and more the energy to play and understand time, with our spiritual creativity recognized in imagination, judgment, and our creation, we dissolve into space.

All literature should give to the reader something to think about, something to help himself and future generations organize their discipline for a better quality of life.

I pass on (fiction today) the discovery that gravity, heat, and light are of the same origin, and I leave the details to be worked out by the following generations. They will explain through evidence an understanding of gravity, heat, and light as the fundamental power to create life and many things more on earth and in the universe through the use of time.

Gravity forms light. The sun, a concentrated power, collects gravity out of space and changes these collected powers through the use of catalysts into heat and light. This represents a reaction of many catalysts which can bring change. This means that gravity and light are of the same origin, only in different conditions.

On earth we can change gravity into light by the use of heat. A burning process represents matter condensed to stone (coal) with the power of gravity, which after a long time will heat when it burns. This means that we change condensed gravity into heat and light—wood represents a catalyst.

We have learned to create light through the use of heat vibrations on catalysts to build our light sources by the use of electricity and other energy.

The following generations will collect all the necessary evidence to prove this reality, to make it understood to all.

God communicates to us through the use of understanding. Through the use of many things we find answers to our questions. Let God speak to you through understanding. Do not disturb Him with selfish questions. God is a power!

Time represents a universal, dimensional power. It consists of contradicting movements expressed in mathematical formulas. Mathematical formulas represent movement or a part of gravity. Matter is expressed through a, b, and c, representing everything related to matter.

$$t = C \begin{matrix} + \\ - \\ : \\ . \end{matrix} \text{ on } \begin{matrix} a \\ b \\ c \end{matrix}$$

Suggestion to read Thought Splinters, one or few pages at a time and then think about a week!